Smartsheet Architecture Solutions

Your Roadmap To Bring Your Smartsheet Project
From Idea To Implementation

By Darren Mullen, the "Smartsheet Guru"

Smart Consulting Services LLC
Tucson, Arizona

Paperback ISBN 979-8-9873987-1-5
eBook ISBN 979-8-9873987-2-2

Library of Congress Control Number: 2023912142

Cover design by Brett Hoffstadt

Dedication

To the Smartsheet Community which has taught me so much.

Acknowledgements

I want to acknowledge and give special thanks to Michael Mulford, Ryan Sides, Mohammed Altaee, and Bill McClellan for reviewing my manuscript and providing valuable feedback. Furthermore, thank you to my book producer, Brett Hoffstadt, for his continued guidance.

Contents

Introduction

Architecting a Smartsheet Solution

Are you wondering how to create a solution in Smartsheet in the most elegant and effective manner? Or, are you using Smartsheet for simple task management, but want to build more complex solutions and are unsure where to start? This book will guide you from an idea through implementation in Smartsheet. Some of the concepts addressed are:

★ Collecting Requirements

★ Identifying the core Smartsheet building blocks

★ Architecting a solution for sharing

★ Documenting the final solution

Getting the Most from this Book

The goal of this book is to give you practical skills to be used in developing a Smartsheet solution from start to finish. First, key concepts will be presented and then an example solution will be built. You are highly encouraged to build out the example solution to get the most benefit. You'll learn a lot more and gain a solid understanding using this hands-on approach.

Example Used in this Book

In order to develop a deeper understanding of the concepts in this book, we'll explore a specific example. A fictitious company, *"Gurus Unlimited,"* has an incentive program for their employees and will be using Smartsheet to keep track of the incentives earned each pay period. Although this example is inspired by a real solution, it has been simplified to better illustrate the concepts presented throughout the book.

While this is one specific example, the concepts covered will be applicable to a multitude of industries and use cases. Here are just some of the applications where Smartsheet is a powerful tool once you become proficient in designing solutions:

- ★ Project management
- ★ Finance
- ★ Accounting
- ★ Customer management
- ★ Product development
- ★ Use your imagination...

Guru Move: Track your task lists in Smartsheet as a way to help you learn Smartsheet's features in a way that is meaningful for you. Very quickly, you'll find yourself experimenting with Smartsheet's full suite of features including reminders and automated workflows. The knowledge you gain will help you identify uses for Smartsheet in more advanced applications. Read ahead to find more "Guru Moves" throughout your journey to architect an effective Smartsheet solution!

Bonus Content

Bonus content has been created for you to enhance and expand the concepts in this book. Throughout the book, you'll see this "Bonus Content" symbol:

This symbol indicates that additional content has been generated to accompany the section in which it appears. Here is the bonus content you will have access to:

- ★ In depth explanation of how to use the INDEX() and MATCH() functions together

- ★ How to create a calendar with the service date anniversary for each employee, updated yearly

- ★ Detailed explanations of the formulas used in the example solution

How do you access this content? You'll be able to access this content after registering on the Smartsheet Guru website using the link shown when you see the bonus content symbol. You are only required to register once and then you'll have access to all of the associated bonus content!

1

Before You Start

Before building a solution in Smartsheet, there are some steps that will take some effort upfront but save time and frustration in the long run. The process presented in this chapter doesn't always prevent having to go back to the drawing board or sending the solution through multiple revisions, but it absolutely helps. Having the discipline to map out the process or problem the solution is intended to solve will allow you to see the end goal as a big picture and apply the tools you have. What you don't want to do is build the solution first and then try to fit your process into it.

1.1 Collect the Requirements

Prior to even mapping out the solution, requirements for the solution should be collected.

Here are some questions we'll address in the book that you'll need to be asking yourself.

★ Who are the key stakeholders?

★ Who are the end users?

★ What problem is the solution going to solve?

★ Who will own the solution?

★ Will the solution be shared exclusively within your organization or externally as well?

1.1.1 *Gurus Unlimited* Requirements

For our example company, *Gurus Unlimited*, the following requirements have been given by the end users:

★ **Human Resources:** HR needs a place to enter employees into Smartsheet and indicate if employees are inactive if they leave the company. HR also wants to maintain a list of incentives available to employees as well as the amount assigned to each incentive. The incentive list should have a way to indicate if the incentives are currently active or inactive because some incentives are turned on and off as business needs dictate.

★ **Managers:** Need to be able to log incentives in Smartsheet for individual employees as they are earned. The incentive log will ask managers when the employee earned the incentive.

★ **Payroll:** See a report by pay period showing which employees have earned incentives and how much. A historical record of the incentives paid to each employee per pay period is required as well. Every employee is on the same biweekly pay period and they are paid the following Friday after the pay period ends. Incentives will be paid based on the pay period in which the incentive is logged by managers, not the date the criteria was met to earn the incentive to allow for additional verification processes before the manager logs the incentive.

★ **Employees:** Each employee will have an individualized dashboard where they can see key information about their employment details and the incentives they have earned. Employees should not have access to data about other employees.

💡 **Guru Move:** Involve key stakeholders and end users early in the development process. When a solution is built out using a top-down approach it is rarely received well by the end users. I have witnessed solutions being built from the top down as well as involving early input from end users and key stakeholders. Can you guess which solutions are received the best by the end users? The ones that involved them in the development process!

1.2 Ownership of the Solution

Smartsheet items need to be owned by a licensed Smartsheet account, so give thought to who or which account will own all of the items. Depending on the size of your organization, the answer to this question may be different. If you are the owner of a small company and the administrator for your organization's Smartsheet account, having everything under your ownership may be sufficient.

For large organizations, concerns about business continuity come into play since employees are more likely to leave without a sense of responsibility to "pass the baton" when they leave. While the ownership of Smartsheet items can be transferred from one account to another, it requires coordination and cooperation between users for the process to go smoothly. For business-critical solutions, creating a licensed service account to own the solution is a way to ensure that ownership of the solution is not tied to one individual.

💡 **Guru Move:** To create a service account, an email address such as "smartsheet@yourcompany.com" can be created and assigned a Smartsheet license. The service account would be the owner of all of the Smartsheet items needed for the solution. A handful of trusted users would have the credentials for the account. For large organizations, the IT department may have a process for creating and storing the credentials for generic accounts. Otherwise, you can use a password vault, such as Zoho Vault, to store and share the credentials with trusted users. See the Additional Resources section at the end of this book to learn more about Zoho Vault.

1.3 Map Out the Solution

After collecting requirements, the next logical step is to create a visual representation of the process based on these requirements. Creating a visual representation of your process will allow you to identify the elements in your tool that can be used to meet each requirement in your process. The graphical format you use will depend on the complexity of the process and how comfortable you are with drawing flowcharts and process maps. If your organization has standardized templates for process maps, use those. Otherwise, you can find resources on process mapping in the format that suits you best from books to online courses. One method to consider is Business Process Modeling and Notation (BPMN). BPMN was created to be a standardized way to document business processes. It is increasingly becoming a best practice to learn and use this method for documenting business processes. See the Additional Resources at the end of this book for more process mapping resources.

1.3.1 *Gurus Unlimited* Process Map

Based on *Gurus Unlimited's* requirements, a process map like the one below can be created using a visual diagram tool, such as Lucidchart. The diagram below does not follow BPMN since not everyone is familiar with BPMN. Also, the example is based on an easy to follow process, so a simple flow chart process map will suffice.

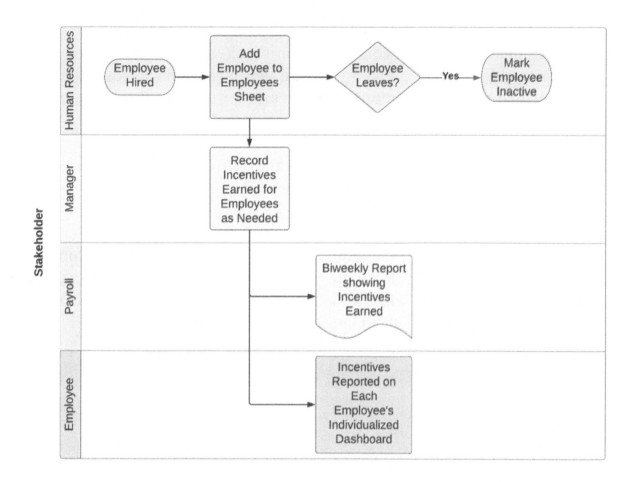

 To learn more about Lucidchart, scan the QR code or visit: smartsheetguru.com/lucidchart

1.4 Isn't There a Smartsheet Template for That?

Congratulations, you've collected your requirements and mapped out your solution. It's time to go find a template that meets your needs. That's all you need to do, correct? Unfortunately, it's not that easy. It if was, consulting agencies such as Smartsheet Guru would have no need to exist!

Templates can be good for learning, but they can cause you to be stuck in a box thinking you have to stay within the bounds of the template. Furthermore, if you want to customize a template it can take longer to reverse engineer the template to make modifications than to build the solution from scratch. Use templates to learn how to apply features, but I suggest developing your solutions from scratch. Not only will you be able to design it to your exact requirements, but you will also be able to easily service the solution since you created every aspect of it and know how each piece works.

2

Identifying the Core Building Blocks Needed

Upon collecting requirements and mapping out the process to be addressed with a Smartsheet solution, you can start identifying the building blocks needed to implement the solution. As a reminder, Smartsheet has 3 core building blocks to use in building your solution:

★ Sheets

★ Reports

★ Dashboards

Let's look at a brief overview of each of the building blocks where we will see some of their features as well as some limitations.*

*Limitations mentioned will be as of the time this book is published. Smartsheet is an ever-evolving platform that continues to release improvements to address limitations experienced by users.

2.1 Sheets

Any Smartsheet solution will contain at least one sheet. However, since you are reading this book you are likely seeking how to architect a solution with multiple sheets. The good news is that sheets can be linked together!

2.1.1 Features of Sheets

Since sheets are the fundamental building blocks in Smartsheet, these are the elements that contain all of the data. A sheet can be used as a simple list of tasks, a small database, a project plan, and more. Sheets are also where automated workflows reside in Smartsheet. Values in cells can be calculated with formulas or brought in from other sheets or sheet summary fields. Sheets have four view types available to help better visualize and manipulate the data contained in the sheet: Grid, Gantt, Card, and Calendar.

2.1.2 Sheet Limitations to be Aware of

As of the publication date of this book, sheets are limited to 500,000 cells and there is a limit of 400 columns and 20,000 rows. The 500,000 cell limit can be made up of any combination of columns and rows before any maximum limits are reached. For example, if you have 50 columns in a sheet then it would be limited to 10,000 rows (50 columns * 10,000 rows = 500,000 cells). Another limit to watch out for in sheets is in regard to cell linking. Sheets are limited to a total of 500,000 inbound links except Smartsheet Gov accounts which are subject to different limits. Before making design decisions based on technical limitations, always check with Smartsheet for the latest limits as they are subject to change.

> **Guru Move:** If you have access to the Smartsheet premium application, DataMesh, there are opportunities to use it to link data between sheets instead of relying on cell linking.

2.2 Reports

Reports are versatile tools useful for enhancing the sharing experience. They can even be used to drive widgets on dashboards. Learning how to properly leverage report features is key to developing a successful Smartsheet solution implementation.

2.2.1 Features of Reports

Reports are sheet-like in appearance but bring some additional special features. The most basic use of a report is to present data from a sheet by selecting specific columns and filter criteria to reduce the amount of information shown. However, reports are more than just a cleaned-up view of a sheet. They can be used to edit data in the underlying sheet, show data from multiple sheets, group rows together, summarize data in columns, and sort the data without affecting the underlying sheet or sheets!

2.2.2 Report Limitations to be Aware of

When sharing a report, viewers of the report will need to have at least the same level of access to the underlying sheet(s) as they are given in the report.* Another limitation to be aware of is when grouping is used. When using the "Group" feature in reports, you will not be able to view more than 2500 rows in the report.

If your organization has access to Smartsheet WorkApps, users can be given access to reports without sharing the underlying sheets.

2.3 Dashboards

Dashboards are used to organize and display data from multiple Smartsheet items and can include data from external sources as well. Additionally, dashboards have widgets to help visualize data from sheets and reports through the use of charts and numerical metric displays.

2.3.1 Features of Dashboards

Dashboards have many useful features beyond just visualizing data. For example, one use of a dashboard is as a portal which can contain links to resources a team requires. A portal can be a collection of links to important Smartsheet items or even external resources like documents in your organization's document management system. Multiple widgets can be added to embed Smartsheet items, such as reports and forms for easy access all in one place.

2.3.2 Dashboard Limitations to be Aware of

The charting features in Smartsheet dashboards are useful, but limited in comparison to what you may be used to in other spreadsheet and charting programs. While Smartsheet dashboards allow embedding items from outside of Smartsheet, such as a YouTube video, the web content widget is limited to content from specific domains.

 For a complete list of approved domains for web content widgets, visit: smartsheetguru.com/webwidgetshelp

2.4 *Gurus Unlimited* Required Smartsheet Items

Taking a look at the process map in 1.3.1, the following items can be immediately identified as required:

- ★ Sheets
    - ☆ Employees Sheet
    - ☆ Incentives Sheet (with a form for managers to enter incentives earned)

- ★ Reports
    - ☆ Report for payroll to show which employees have earned incentives in the pay period.

- ★ Dashboards
    - ☆ An individualized dashboard for each employee

What items will be needed, but aren't apparent from the process map? Let's think about this before building out a solution. HR requested the ability to maintain a list of incentives and the amount of each incentive. This can turn into a lookup sheet for the incentives sheet as well. To meet the biweekly report for payroll there will need to be a way of tracking the biweekly pay periods and pay dates. A good way to do this will be in a separate sheet. Payroll also wants a historical record of the incentives earned by each employee every two weeks, so there will also need to be a sheet to archive all of the incentives earned each pay period.

When it comes to creating the individualized dashboard for each employee while maintaining their privacy, this will require that there is a way to display an employee's unique data on a unique dashboard without risking the employee's data being seen by other employees. A great way to do this is to have a sheet created for each employee that will then be used to pull in unique data about the employee to display on their unique dashboard. In order to make the process scalable for new employees, it should be simple to copy a template with the sheet and dashboard, then set the sheet to pull in the employee's data.

With these ideas in mind, the following additional items will be required:

- ★ Sheets
  - ☆ A sheet to list each incentive, its amount, and its current status (active or inactive)
  - ☆ A sheet to archive the incentives paid every two weeks
  - ☆ A sheet to calculate the current pay period data (pay period start, end, and pay date)
  - ☆ A sheet for each employee will be needed to pull in their incentive data in order to display it on their individualized dashboard

Now, have all the items been identified? Maybe. We may find during the build process that an item was forgotten, or a new feature may be asked for that wasn't accounted for in the initial requirement gathering. However, what has been identified is a good start.

3

Organizational Structure: Workspaces and Folders

Now that you've identified the core building blocks to be used in your solution, you'll want to think about how to organize all of the items in your solution. Smartsheet has two ways to organize your sheets, reports, and dashboards. Organization is achieved through the use of workspaces and folders. Chances are you will use at least one workspace with some folders underneath it, but you may have to use multiple workspaces for reasons discussed later in this book. Both have the same rules regarding what items they can contain as shown in this graphic.

 Can Contain
- Sheets, reports, dashboards
- Folders

 Cannot Contain
- Workspaces

So, what is the difference between workspaces and folders? Features. Folders can contain Smartsheet items but have no other features. Workspaces, on the other hand, can be shared and customized with a unique logo and color scheme.

3.1 Workspaces and Folders as Template Sets

Remember when I said to shy away from using templates? One nuance, I wasn't referring to templates that you create yourself! Both workspaces and folders can be used to create a template set, which is a collection of sheets, reports, and dashboards. The template set can then be replicated to consistently create the same set of Smartsheet items for a specific purpose. When this is done, any links between sheets are maintained. For example, it is customary to have a metrics sheet that pulls data from a project plan. If a template set includes such a sheet, any cell links or ranges in formulas will be replicated within the context of the new set of sheets! A common application of this is to create a template set for a project which would at least include a project schedule, reports based on the schedule, and a project dashboard.

When deciding whether to use a folder or workspace to create a template set, think about the end use of the items you will create from the template set. Ask the question:

★ Will the new items require a different set of sharing permissions?

   ☆ If so, a workspace is the best bet as you can easily copy the template workspace then share the new workspace with new collaborators.

   ☆ If you will be replicating the template set and the new items will have the same sharing permissions or you will need to replicate the template set into another workspace, then using a folder to contain the template set is the proper choice.

Guru Move: Why not have the best of both worlds? Create a template workspace then a folder immediately under it. The folder will contain all of the items for the template while the workspace itself will hold the folder. This way you can choose to replicate the workspace (including the folder under it) or just the folder if desired!

3.2 *Gurus Unlimited* Organizational Structure

In the context of the solution being built for *Gurus Unlimited*, what organizational structure will be used? If you said "both" you are correct. This solution will ultimately utilize multiple workspaces and folders. Furthermore, for the employee dashboards a template set will need to be created to make the creation of dashboards for each employee consistent and scalable. Our example solution will benefit from two workspaces.

★ **Administration Workspace:** This workspace will hold the Smartsheet items containing data on all employees such as the sheets containing employee data, incentives, and payroll reports hold sensitive information that should only be accessed by a limited number of employees at *Gurus Unlimited*. A separate workspace with these administrative items is the best way to ensure that the data is only shared with the trusted employees.

★ **Employee Dashboard Workspace:** The individualized sheets and dashboards for each employee can be contained in a separate workspace for easier sharing with a broader audience. For example, lower-level managers will need to have access to all of the employee dashboards to administer the incentive program, but do not need to be shared to the Administration workspace. This workspace will also contain a template set in the form of a folder with the necessary items for creating each employee's individualized dashboard.

Chapter 5 will expand more on the folder structure for these workspaces.

4

Architecting Solutions for Sharing

A key feature of Smartsheet is its collaborative work features. This means that Smartsheet is built for sharing. However, sometimes you don't want to share EVERYTHING in a solution. For example, maybe you want to have external suppliers or customers view and even interact with the data in Smartsheet. However, you may not want these external parties to have access to all of the data. Similarly, you may want specific data shared internally within your organization to a broad audience while a limited set of employees will be given access to all of the items in a solution. When designing a solution for sharing, here are some key questions to ask:

★ Will the end users have Smartsheet accounts?

★ Will the end users need only view access to the data or need the ability to edit it as well?

★ What Smartsheet tools do you have available? Are you limited to the features in core Smartsheet, or do you have access to Smartsheet's premium apps?

4.1 Options for Sharing

Some sharing methods require users to have Smartsheet accounts while others allow anyone to view a Smartsheet item. Furthermore, Smartsheet items can be shared individually or through workspaces.

4.1.1 Smartsheet Account Requirements

If users are shared to a Smartsheet item by entering their email address, they will need to have a Smartsheet account. A Smartsheet license is not required for the end users if all they require is the ability to view or make simple edits to the item. In this case, a free Smartsheet account will do.

If it is desired for end users to not be required to have a Smartsheet account, then items can be shared using the publish feature. This should only be done for items that contain data that is truly public as anyone that gains access to the link for the published item can view it.

4.1.2 Sharing Workspaces and Individual Items

Workspaces can be used to control sharing at a high level. Let's say you have specific Smartsheet items that you want to share to a broad audience. You could simply put any Smartsheet items needing to be shared into this workspace. The workspace can then be shared with the users needing access at the appropriate permission level.

However, there are many instances where this type of sharing doesn't fit the use case. There may be specific sheets, reports, and dashboards that need to be shared with a user or users who don't need full access to a workspace. In this scenario, you can share Smartsheet items individually with each user that needs access instead of the entire workspace.

Guru Move: If you find that you are always sharing items to the same group of Smartsheet users, consider creating a Smartsheet Group. For example, you may find that you always need to share items with all employees in payroll or HR. Creating a group with these users expedites sharing and prevents leaving someone out. Note that only Smartsheet users identified as "System Admins" or "Group Admins" can create groups. If you don't fulfill one of these roles, you'll have to find one of these admins in your organization.

4.2 Report Sharing Considerations

Reports are great for sharing a filtered view of a sheet or aggregating data from multiple sheets. However, remember from 2.2.2 that users shared to a report will need to have at least the same level of access to the source sheet(s) as they are given to a report. For example, if a user needs edit access to a report, they will also need edit access to the source sheet(s).

In use cases with users internal to your organization, this may not be a problem, but if you wish a report to be shared with a large audience or users external to your organization, this may not be desirable. In this situation, there are a few options:

★ Create a sheet and report containing only the data intended to be shared with the target audience

☆ This option works if the data can easily be separated into individual sheets for each audience.

★ Publish the report

☆ Remember that anyone that gains the link to the published item can view it, so use this option with great care!

★ Send the report as an attachment

☆ The report can be sent as an attachment one time or on a recurring schedule. The attachment can be sent in either PDF or

Excel format. When choosing the PDF attachment format, you have the option to include or hide comments!

4.2.1 Alternatives to Reports for Sharing Filtered Data

If you have access to Smartsheet's Dynamic View, then this creates far greater opportunities. A Dynamic View can be built with a source that is either a sheet or a report. The benefit of using Dynamic View is that the source sheets and reports do not need to be shared with the end users and they can even be given access to edit data. Furthermore, Dynamic View can be used to allow end users to only edit specific columns! Like reports, Dynamic Views can be filtered based on the logged in user.

For users that have an Enterprise Smartsheet plan with access to Smartsheet WorkApps, then you have the ability to share a report to end users without needing to share the report itself. You can even give the users the ability to edit data in the report without sharing the source sheet(s) with them! Users that are shared to WorkApps do not need to be in your organization and don't need an Enterprise plan either. Another benefit of Smartheet WorkApps is that you can create custom user roles with varying levels of access to Smarthseet items added to the WorkApp.

4.3 *Gurus Unlimited* Sharing Architecture

For the solution being built for *Gurus Unlimited*, the items in the solution will only be shared internally within the organization and all end users will have a Smartsheet account. Therefore, the solution can be developed to utilize the workspace and item sharing capabilities.

In 3.2 it was determined that two workspaces will be required, and they will be shared as follows:

★ **Administration Workspace** - The entire administration workspace can be shared to a limited number of employees who will be responsible for maintaining the items contained in this workspace. If any additional employees require access to a limited set of these items, they can be shared as needed.

★ **Employee Dashboard Workspace** - The employee dashboard workspace will be shared to any management employees that will oversee the creation of new dashboards. Each of the individualized dashboards that are created can then be shared to the respective employees.

5

Building the Solution

Upon completion of the methods in the previous chapters, it's now time to get into Smartsheet and start building! This chapter will give an overview of some of the methodologies used when building a solution as well as a hands-on walkthrough of how to build the *Gurus Unlimited* solution.

5.1 Building Methodology

The methodology for building out a Smartsheet solution will vary depending on the complexity and the developer(s) implementing it. However, here are some high-level guidelines:

- ★ Create the workspaces required

- ★ Identify the sheets that will be the key building blocks and start with those

- ★ Create the remaining items and any templates needed

- ★ Check that the solution meets the defined requirements

- ★ Test the solution with the end users and make incremental improvements based on feedback

★ For complex solutions, it is advisable to break the build into modules and thoroughly test each module instead of taking on the entire build in one pass

5.2 Handling Additional Feature Requests

Inevitably when the end users start testing the solution, new features will be requested. Don't take this as a failure of your build process as it is a natural part of launching a new solution. A couple reasons why this happens are that requirements are left out during the initial collection process or users see how powerful the solution is and want to add even more functionality. New features generally fall into two categories:

★ Features that will change the underlying architecture

★ Add-on features to enhance the existing architecture

How do you identify which category a new feature falls into? There is some subjectivity, but a good guideline is to consider if implementing the new feature could potentially impact or break the functionality of the current solution. If implementation of the new feature could impact current functionally, it is likely a change to the underlying architecture. Otherwise, it's an add-on feature. Let's see some examples of each of these.

5.2.1 Features that will Change the Underlying Architecture

Changes to the underlying architecture can result in tedious updates once the solution is launched. Since this book is about building new solutions, we won't discuss the challenges or methodology for changing the architecture of a solution that is launched and actively being used. Except to say that it will require careful planning and extensive testing to ensure that all previous functionally is still intact!

The good news is that the best time to implement a change to the underlying architecture is in the midst of creating the solution before it is launched! So what are some examples of changes to the underlying architecture?

★ Data collection requirements that require new sheets and cross-sheet linking

★ Introducing 3rd party integrations that will require changing how data is stored in Smartsheet

★ Changes to templates

★ A change to the unique identifier used for linking records across sheets

In summary, do what you can to identify any potential changes to the architecture before launching the solution. A strategic way to do this is testing the solution with a large cross-section of end users. From their testing, you'll get feedback on useability and shake out any requirements that were identified originally.

5.2.2 Add-on Features to Enhance the Existing Architecture

Features that add additional functionality to the existing architecture are the easiest to implement as they will likely not break any existing functionality. That's not to say they are always without risks, but the potential risks, if any, should be minimal. The good news here is that these features are much less critical to identify before the solution is launched. What are some examples?

★ Adding additional reports for filtering and sorting data

★ 3rd party integrations that simply read data in Smartsheet or do not require changing how the data is stored

★ Calculating new metrics from data that already exists in the solution

★ Adding a document builder mapping that doesn't require new columns

The list above is nowhere near exhaustive but should give you ideas of features that won't require changing the underlying architecture. When these types of feature requests come up, take them as an opportunity to shine. In these situations, you can really show off the rich feature set of Smartsheet without being too concerned with breaking the current solution. Don't be too casual with small changes, however. Fully testing these new features should still be in your plan!

5.3 *Gurus Unlimited* Solution Build

The moment you've been waiting for: building the solution! A quick note before we begin. All of the formulas and dates shown in this example solution are based on a Smartsheet account using the regional preferences of "English (United States)" as defined in the account's "Personal Settings." The functions used in the formulas will be the same, but the difference is in the use of commas (,) and semicolons (;) depending on your regional preferences. All dates are shown in the format of MM/DD/YY. Please keep this in mind if you are in a region that uses a different format for either of these.

How do we build out the *Gurus Unlimited* solution? Per our guidelines, the logical first step when building a solution is to create the workspaces that will contain all of the items to be used in the Smartsheet solution. Remember from Chapter 3 that the solution will contain two workspaces.

Let's create the workspaces then fill them with all the required items! Let's give the two workspaces descriptive identifiers. They will be called "Gurus Unlimited Administration" and "Gurus Unlimited Employee Dashboards." The workspaces can then be populated with the appropriate items.

> ▸ 😕 Gurus Unlimited Administration

> ▸ 😕 Gurus Unlimited Employee Dashboards

5.3.1 The Administration Workspace

Within the *Gurus Unlimited* Administration workspace there will be 3 folders for organization:

⭐ **Employee Data**: Will contain the employee sheet

⭐ **Incentives**: Will contain the sheet used to collect the incentives earned by each employee and any additional sheets related to incentives

⭐ **Payroll**: Will contain pay period data and the report to be used by payroll

5.3.1.1. The Employee Data Folder

The "Employee Data" folder will contain a single sheet named "Employees." This is the perfect sheet to start with since it will contain the foundational data for the rest of the solution.

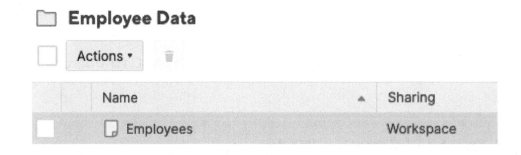

Below is a snippet of the "Employees" sheet with sample data already loaded. The sample data is taken from the Microsoft Northwind Traders database which is a database of fictitious information.

Forms   Employees ☆

Employee Full Name	Employee ID	Status	First Name	Last Name	Role	Email	Hire Date
Nancy Freehafer	EID-0001	Active	Nancy	Freehafer	Sales Representative	nancy@northwin	08/01/22
Andrew Cencini	EID-0002	Active	Andrew	Cencini	Sales Representative	andrew@northwi	06/13/22
Jan Kotas	EID-0003	Active	Jan	Kotas	Sales Representative	jan@northwindtr:	12/05/22
Mariya Sergienko	EID-0004	Active	Mariya	Sergienko	Solution Architect	mariya@northwir	02/01/22
Steven Thorpe	EID-0005	Active	Steven	Thorpe	Solution Architect	steven@northwir	11/28/22
Michael Neipper	EID-0006	Active	Michael	Neipper	Financial Analyst	michael@northw	08/02/21
Robert Zare	EID-0007	Active	Robert	Zare	Financial Analyst	robert@northwin	03/07/22
Laura Giussani	EID-0008	Active	Laura	Giussani	Financial Analyst	laura@northwind	08/29/22
Anne Hellung-Larse	EID-0009	Active	Anne	Hellung-Larse	Financial Analyst	anne@northwind	08/15/22
Anna Bedecs	EID-0010	Active	Anna	Bedecs	Solution Architect	anna@northwind	08/01/22
Antonio Gratacos S	EID-0011	Active	Antonio	Gratacos Sols	Solution Architect	antonio@northwi	06/13/22
Thomas Axen	EID-0012	Active	Thomas	Axen	Purchasing Representative	thomas@northwi	12/05/22

Let's discuss some key points about this sheet. First, notice the "Employee ID" column. This will be an important column as it is used to create a unique identifier for each employee. What the ID looks like isn't that important, the important point is that it needs to be unique for each employee. I can't stress how important this is when designing a solution that will require data to be referenced across multiple sheets. What is being done here is creating a type of relational database where the "Employee ID" is the key for each record. It is highly advisable to use an identifier that will never need to change. Names and email addresses can change with the most frequent examples being a woman changing her last name upon marriage or a man named "Robert" deciding he wants to go by the nickname "Bob" instead. When using a unique identifier such as the "Employee ID" for cross-sheet linking, any lookup formulas will not be affected if an employee's name or email address changes over time.

Also notice that the "Employees Full Name" column has a column formula applied. It is simply a formula that concatenates each employee's first and last name. When designing a solution that requires rows to be identified by something like a combination of a first and last name, it is much easier to design the solution with the first and last names in separate columns. This is because it is easy to concatenate the columns, but harder to split the full name column apart into first and last name columns if needed because of variations in the format of names. For example, names may contain multiple spaces or hyphens and this is hard to account for in a simple formula. For reference, here is the column formula in the "Employee Full Name" column.

Employee Full Name f_x	Employee ID	Status	First Name	Last Name
=[First Name]@row + " " + [Last Name]@row		Active	Nancy	Freehafer

Remember that HR wants to have the ability to mark employee's as active or inactive? The Employee sheet meets that requirement through the use of the dropdown column named "Status."

Display employee
service anniversaries
on a calendar

smartsheetguru.com/architecture-bonus

5.3.1.2 The Incentives Folder

With the "Employees" sheet created and filled with employee data, the next key part of the solution revolves around Incentives. The requirements are:

★ A list of incentives with the incentive amount and a way to indicate if the incentives are currently active or inactive

★ A sheet for managers to log when an employee earns an incentive

With these requirements in mind, there will be two sheets contained in this folder.

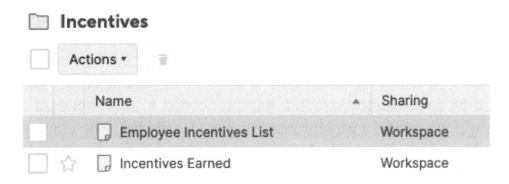

5.3.1.2.1 Employee Incentives List

In 2.4 it was mentioned that the list of incentives could be used as a lookup sheet, so that should ideally be created before creating the sheet that will be used for logging the incentives. What should the incentives sheet look like? It will be very simple as shown below.

The "Incentive" column is the name of the incentive while the "Incentive Amount" column assigns a monetary value to the incentive and the "Status" column can be used to mark the incentive as currently active or inactive. Notice the column "Incentive ID" which is an auto number column. Why is this column important? Remember this sheet will be used as a lookup sheet, so a unique identifier should be assigned to each row. This will be handy in case the name of the incentive needs to be changed at some point in the future.

5.3.1.2.2 Incentives Earned

Next on the list of requirements is a sheet for managers to log incentives earned by each employee. What will be needed in this sheet? At a minimum there will need to be a way for managers to identify both the employee that has earned an incentive and the incentive. Since both the "Employees" and "Employee Incentives List" lookup sheets have unique row identifiers, these are the best values for managers to use to identify both of these uniquely and reliably for cross-sheet linking. Also, thinking about reporting it will be nice to have the employee's name, the date the incentive was earned, as well as the name and dollar amount of the incentive earned. At this point, the sheet will look like this:

The primary column is the "Employee Full Name" column because it will be useful for grouping incentives earned by employees in reports generated from this sheet. Based on the Employee ID and the Incentive ID, the rest of the fields in the "Incentives Earned" sheet can be filled out using cross-sheet formulas.

Remember that a form will be needed for this sheet so that managers can easily log incentives for employees. The form will be very simple and consist of 3 fields to minimize the amount of data entry needed. See the form below with sample data in the "Employee ID," "Incentive ID," and "Date Earned" fields.

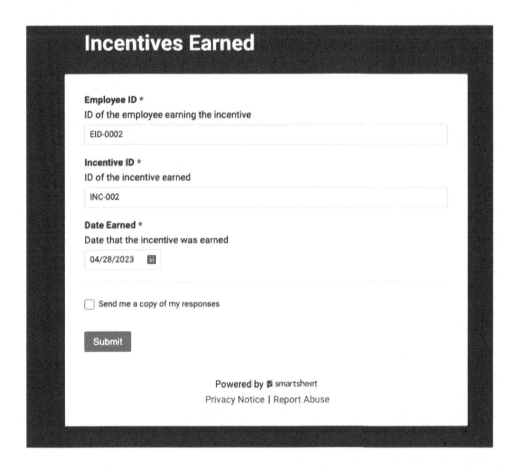

> 💡 **Guru Move:** Keeping a form as simple as possible and presenting only the fields relevant for the submitter is a good design principle. Conditional logic in forms can be used to accomplish this for complex forms.

Let's see what the "Incentives Earned" sheet looks like after submitting the form with the sample data.

Employee Full Name	Employee ID	Date Earned	Incentive ID	Incentive	Incentive Amount	Incentive Submitted Date
	EID-0002	04/28/23	INC-002			05/01/23 3:40 PM

In order to fill out the rest of the fields, some cross-sheet formulas will be needed. First, we'll take a look at the result, then how to get there.

Employee Full Name	Employee ID	Date Earned	Incentive ID	Incentive	Incentive Amount
Andrew Cencini	EID-0002	04/28/23	INC-002	Employee Referral	$500.00

You'll notice 3 column formulas have been added. All of the formulas are cross-sheet formulas that utilize the Smartsheet functions INDEX() and MATCH(). Let's look at the formulas in each column.

Employee Full Name

`=INDEX({Employees | Employee Full Name}, MATCH([Employee ID]@row, {Employees | Employee ID}, 0))`

Incentive

`=INDEX({Employee Incentives List | Incentive}, MATCH([Incentive ID]@row, {Employee Incentives List | Incentive ID}))`

Incentive Amount

Incentive ID	Incentive	Incentive Amount	Incentive Submitted Date	💬
	fx	*fx*		
INC-002	Employee Referral	=INDEX({Employee Incentives List | Incentive Amount}, MATCH([Incentive ID]@row, {Employee Incentives List | Incentive ID}))		

💡 **Guru Move:** If you've ever created a cross-sheet reference in Smartsheet, you'll know that a default name is assigned in the format [Source Sheet Name] Range [#]. In the "Employee Full Name" column formula the default name would be "Employees Range 1". However, this type of name isn't very descriptive, so it is nice to give the range a name with more meaning. A suggested naming convention for ranges is:

[Source Sheet Name] | [Column Name in the Source Sheet]

Using this pattern, the name of the range referencing the "Employee Full Name" column in the "Employees" sheet is, "Employees | Employee Full Name". You'll notice this same cross-sheet range naming convention throughout the formulas in this book.

Using INDEX() and MATCH() together.

smartsheetguru.com/architecture-bonus

5.3.1.3 The Payroll Folder

With the sheets containing the employee and incentive data created, the requirements for payroll can now start to be met. As a reminder, the requirements for payroll are:

Payroll: See a report by pay period showing which employees have earned incentives and how much and have a historical record of the incentives paid to each employee per pay period. The pay period details are that every employee is on the same biweekly pay period, and they are paid the following Friday after the pay period ends.

Section 2.4 identified that the items needed for payroll are as follows:

★ A sheet to calculate the current pay period data (pay period start, end, and pay date)

★ A sheet to archive the incentives paid every two weeks

★ A report for payroll to show which employees have earned incentives in the pay period.

5.3.1.3.1 Pay Period Metadata

Since the sheet to calculate the current pay period will be used as a lookup sheet, it is best to start with this building block in the "Payroll" folder. Let's name the sheet "Pay Period Metadata" and it will look like this:

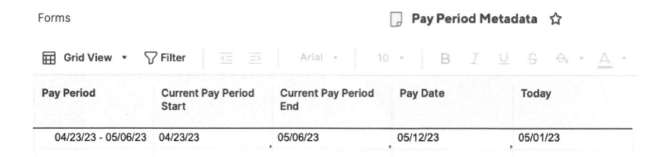

Pay Period	Current Pay Period Start	Current Pay Period End	Pay Date	Today
04/23/23 - 05/06/23	04/23/23	05/06/23	05/12/23	05/01/23

The primary column is named "Pay Period" and is a concatenation of the columns "Current Pay Period Start" and "Current Pay Period End." The "Pay Date" column is the date in which the earnings from the current pay period will be paid to employees. You may be wondering why there is also a column called "Today." This was added because formulas in this sheet rely on the TODAY() function, and the function TODAY() will not update to the correct date each day unless there is activity in the sheet every day. Therefore, the column "Today" has been added along with an automated workflow to update the date in the "Today" column. The workflow is simple and is shown here.

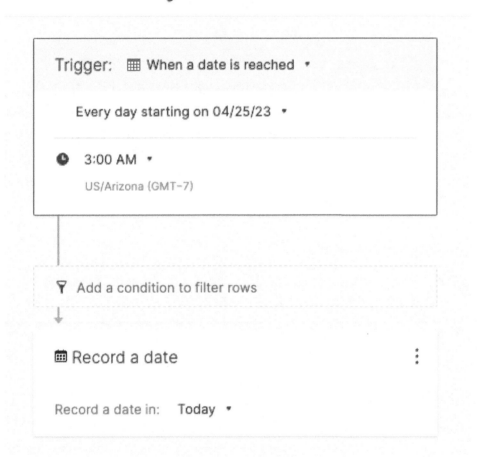

The workflow simply runs at 3:00 AM every day and records the current date in the "Today" column. This is enough to force the TODAY() function to update with the current date.

One more thing before I show the formulas used in the calculations. Since these formulas will calculate the new pay period start, end, and pay dates every two weeks, they will need a reference to start from. Payroll has provided the first pay period start date in the year of 2023, which was Sunday, Jan-01-2023. This is the reference we need and for convenience has been entered into the "Pay Period Metadata" as a sheet summary.

Sheet Summary :

Initial Pay Period Start

01/01/23

This sheet summary field will be referenced in the date calculation formulas on this sheet. Alternatively, the initial date could have been entered directly into each of the formulas, but using a sheet summary keeps the formulas less complex and easier to read. Let's now take a look at the formulas used to calculate the values for the "Current Pay Period Start," "Current Pay Period End," and "Pay Date" columns.

Current Pay Period Start

Pay Period	Current Pay Period Start	Current Pay Period End	Pay Date	Today
04/23/23 - 05/06/23	=(INT((TODAY() - [Initial Pay Period Start]#) / 14) * 14) + [Initial Pay Period Start]#			

Current Pay Period End

Pay Period	Current Pay Period Start	Current Pay Period End	Pay Date	Today
04/23/23 - 05/06/23	04/23/23	=[Current Pay Period Start]@row + 13		05/01/23

Pay Date

Pay Period	Current Pay Period Start	Current Pay Period End	Pay Date	Today
04/23/23 - 05/06/23	04/23/23	05/06/23	=[Current Pay Period End]@row + 6	

💡 **Guru Move:** Sheet summary fields can be used in sheet formulas. Reference them using the syntax [Sheet Summary Field Name]#. Notice that the "#" replaces the row number or @row operator used when referencing sheet columns in formulas.

Explanation of the formulas used in the Pay Period Metadata Sheet

smartsheetguru.com/architecture-bonus

5.3.1.3.2 Archiving the Incentives Every Two Weeks

With the "Pay Period Metadata" sheet out of the way, focus can now be turned to the sheet which will be used to archive the incentives paid every two weeks. First of all, why is this sheet needed? Couldn't payroll just run a report on the "Incentives Earned" sheet and look for incentives earned in the pay period for the next upcoming pay date? They could, but that would require manually sorting through the sheet, changing sheet filters, or creating a report that needs its filters updated every two weeks. While this would theoretically work, it is error prone due to the manual nature of changing the sheet filters.

> 💡 **Guru Move:** When designing a solution, always look for opportunities to reduce errors. It can take a little more effort upfront, but the time saved by avoiding even one error in reporting data will make it worthwhile. Pitching it in this way to stakeholders will usually result in quick buy-in.

Now, you may be scratching your head wondering how this will be accomplished. How do we go from a log of incentives in the "Incentives Earned" sheet to a sheet listing each of the incentives earned every two weeks? And in an automated manner? The word *automated* should be a hint that an automated workflow will be needed.

When designing solutions in Smartsheet, there is usually more than one way to accomplish a task. I say this because archiving the biweekly data could be accomplished in multiple ways. For our example solution, we will choose to employ a method that will use the "Employees" sheet to help in this biweekly archival process. In order to do this, we will add columns to the "Employees" sheet to pull in the pay period data as well as the incentives earned based on the employee's ID and the current pay period. An automated workflow then runs at the end of the day on the last day of the pay period to archive the incentives earned for each employee. This is hard to visualize in just words, so we'll first start with the additional columns added to the "Employees" sheet.

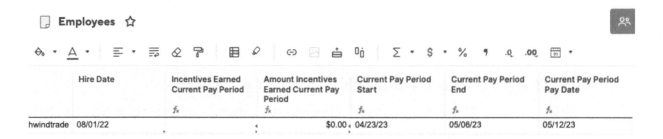

All of the columns to the right of the "Hire Date" column have been added for this purpose. Furthermore, some sheet summaries have been added to help with the pay period formulas.

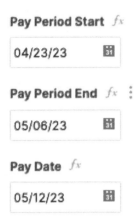

What are the formulas used to calculate these sheet summaries? Cross-sheet references are being used to bring in these dates from the "Pay Period Metadata" sheet. Sheet Summary fields don't have an option in their menu for cell linking, but you can effectively create your own cell link using a cross-sheet reference. Below are what the formulas in these summary fields look like.

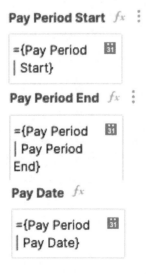

> 💡 **Guru Move:** You can use cross-sheet references to a single cell in another sheet in summary fields. In order to do this, you need to start a formula such as "=if(" then the tooltip will show the link "Reference Another Sheet." After clicking on this link, you can create your cross-sheet reference and it will be inserted into your summary field. Just make sure to delete the "if(" and leave only the "=" before the cross-sheet reference in the form ={Cross-Sheet Reference Name}.

Below are each of the additional columns added along with a description of their purpose and the column formulas used in each.

Incentives Earned Current Pay Period - Searches the "Incentives Earned" sheet and looks for rows that match the employee ID with a submitted date within the current pay period range. It then creates a comma separated list with the names of the incentives that were logged by a manager for a particular employee during the current pay period.

Incentives Earned Current Pay Period	Amount Incentives Earned Current Pay Period	Current Pay Period Start	Current Pay Period End	Current Pay Period Pay Date	
f_x	f_x	f_x	f_x	f_x	

`=JOIN(COLLECT({Incentives Earned | Incentive}, {Incentives Earned | Employee ID}, [Employee ID]@row, {Incentives Earned | Created}, AND(@cell >= [Current Pay Period Start]@row, @cell <= [Current Pay Period End]@row)), ",")`

Amount Incentives Earned Current Pay Period - Similar to the "Incentives Earned Current Pay Period" column except that this column sums the amount of incentives that were logged by a manager for a particular employee during the current pay period.

Incentives Earned Current Pay Period	Amount Incentives Earned Current Pay Period	Current Pay Period Start	Current Pay Period End	Current Pay Period Pay Date	
f_x	f_x	f_x	f_x	f_x	

`=SUMIFS({Incentives Earned | Incentive Amount}, {Incentives Earned | Employee ID}, [Employee ID]@row, {Incentives Earned | Created}, AND(@cell >= [Current Pay Period Start]@row, @cell <= [Current Pay Period End]@row))`

Current Pay Period Start - The date that the current pay period starts, taken from the associated sheet summary field.

Incentives Earned Current Pay Period	Amount Incentives Earned Current Pay Period	Current Pay Period Start	Current Pay Period End	Current Pay Period Pay Date	
f_x	f_x	f_x	f_x	f_x	
	$0.00	=[Pay Period Start]#	05/06/23	05/12/23	

Current Pay Period End - The date that the current pay period ends, taken from the associated sheet summary field.

Incentives Earned Current Pay Period	Amount Incentives Earned Current Pay Period	Current Pay Period Start	Current Pay Period End	Current Pay Period Pay Date	
f_x	f_x	f_x	f_x	f_x	
	$0.00	04/23/23	=[Pay Period End]#	05/12/23	

Current Pay Period Pay Date - The pay date associated with the current pay period, taken from the associated sheet summary field.

Incentives Earned Current Pay Period	Amount Incentives Earned Current Pay Period	Current Pay Period Start	Current Pay Period End	Current Pay Period Pay Date	
f_x	f_x	f_x	f_x	f_x	
	$0.00	04/23/23	05/06/23	=[Pay Date]#	

If you remember, an entry was made in the "Incentives Earned" sheet for an employee with an employee ID of EID-0002 (Andrew Cencini) and an incentive ID of INC-002 (Employee Referral). Let's see what these formulas brought in for this incentive.

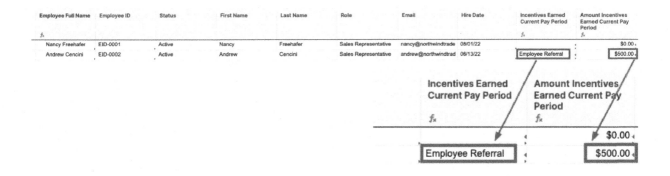

Explanation of the incentives formulas used in the Employees Sheet

smartsheetguru.com/architecture-bonus

Now that the Employees sheet is bringing in the data for the current pay period, we can think about how to archive this data at the appropriate time. Before creating the automated workflow, a destination sheet will be required. A new sheet will be created in the "Payroll" folder and called "Biweekly Incentives Earned." This sheet will be receiving rows from the "Employees" sheet. Since the columns from the "Employees Sheet" will be copied into the "Biweekly Incentives Earned" sheet, all that is needed in this destination sheet is the primary column, and it can be renamed "Employee Full Name" to match the primary column in the "Employees" sheet. All other default columns automatically added when the "Biweekly Incentives Earned" sheet is created can be deleted. It should now look like this:

| Forms | | | | | | | Biweekly Incentives Earned ☆ |

| ⊞ Grid View ▾ | ▽ Filter | ⇽ ⇾ | Arial ▾ | 10 ▾ | B I U S |

Employee Full Name

Returning to the Employees sheet, a new automated workflow can be created. Give it a descriptive name such as "Copy Incentives Earned Biweekly" indicating this will be an automated workflow to copy rows. The trigger will be when a date is reached using the date field "Current Pay Period End." Choose a time on this day when no more entries will be made. In *Gurus Unlimited's* case, managers will not be entering new incentives late on a Saturday night, so 10:00 PM was chosen as the time for the automation to run.

Let's add a filter condition to check that the amount of the incentive earned on a given row is greater than zero. This ensures that only the rows for employees that were actually awarded an incentive during the pay period will be copied to the archive sheet. The action chosen will be "Copy rows" with the destination being the archive sheet named "Biweekly Incentives Earned."

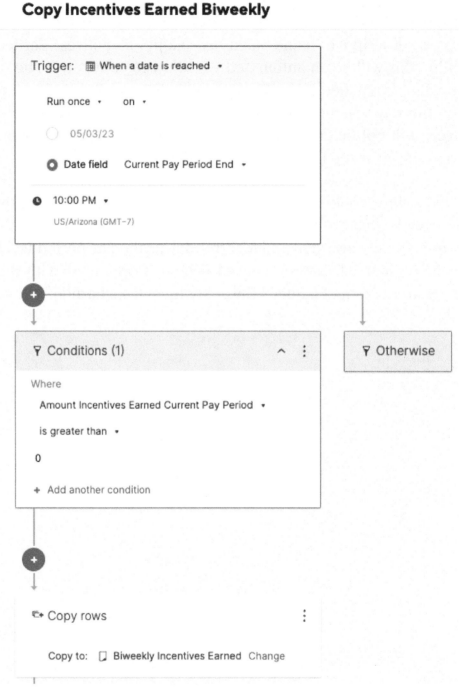

When creating a workflow like this, you may want to test the result immediately and not have to wait until the date in the column "Current Pay Period End." Thankfully, Smartsheet has a feature that can be used to run a workflow immediately. Simply click on the kebab (3 vertical dot) menu associated with the workflow to be tested and choose "Run now..."

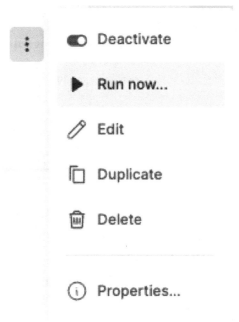

The following dialog window will appear. You can choose to trigger the workflow on all rows in the sheet or select specific rows by row number. We'll keep it simple and choose to trigger the workflow on the entire sheet.

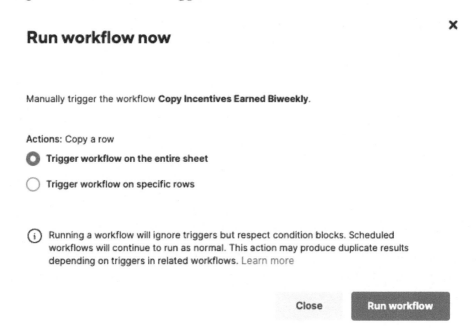

After clicking the "Run workflow" button, you'll receive a confirmation if the run was successful and can now take a look at the destination sheet, "Biweekly Incentives Earned."

The screenshot above does not show all the columns in the sheet but notice that this sheet now contains a copy of the matching row from the "Employees" sheet. With the archive sheet and the automated workflow setup, the next step will be to produce a report for payroll showing only the incentives that are due to be paid at any given time.

5.3.1.3.3 Creating the Payroll Report

Before the report can be created showing the new upcoming pay period, we must have a way to identify the rows for the report. To do so, a column named "Include in Payroll Report" will be added as a checkbox. Then, a column formula will check to see if the "Current Pay Period Pay Date" is the most recent date and check all rows that match this condition.

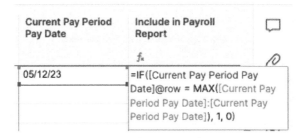

The formula identifies the most recent pay date using the MAX() function and checks if the date in the "Current Pay Period Pay Date" column matches. If the dates match, then this row belongs to the current pay period and the box is checked.

With that column added, the payroll report can be created, and it will show only the rows for the next upcoming pay date based on the column "Include in Payroll Report" being checked.

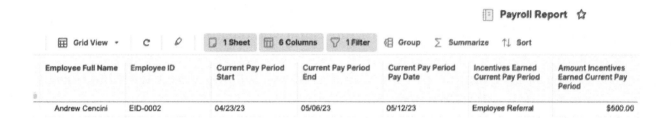

5.3.2 The Employee Dashboards Workspace

For the workspace, "Gurus Unlimited Employee Dashboards" a single folder named "Employee Dashboard Template" will be created. This folder will serve as a template set and will contain the necessary items to create the unique employee dashboards for each employee.

This folder will contain two items, namely a sheet named "Employee File" and a dashboard named "Employee Dashboard."

5.3.2.1 Employee File

In section 2.4 we identified that in order to create the unique, individualized dashboard for each employee, there will also need to be a unique sheet to pull in their incentive data in order to display it on their individualized dashboard. The "Employee File" sheet will fill this need and will contain the columns necessary to collect the data for the employee dashboard.

Below is an example of an employee file sheet populated with data based on the Employee ID, EID-002.

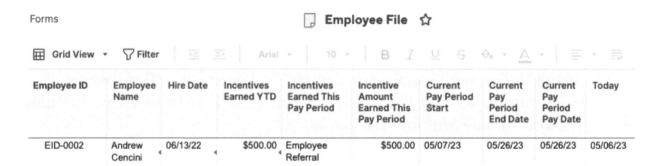

Employee ID	Employee Name	Hire Date	Incentives Earned YTD	Incentives Earned This Pay Period	Incentive Amount Earned This Pay Period	Current Pay Period Start	Current Pay Period End Date	Current Pay Period Pay Date	Today
EID-0002	Andrew Cencini	06/13/22	$500.00	Employee Referral	$500.00	05/07/23	05/26/23	05/26/23	05/06/23

The column "Employee ID" will be used to pull in the data for the "Employee Name" through the "Incentive Amount Earned This Pay Period" columns. The columns "Current Pay Period Start," "Current Pay Period End Date," and "Current Pay Period Pay Date" are linked directly from the corresponding cells in the "Pay Period Metadata" sheet using Smartsheet's cell linking feature. The "Today" column is again being populated with an automated workflow. For reference, the formulas used for the "Employee Name" through the "Incentive Amount Earned This Pay Period" columns are below. Notice that INDEX() and MATCH() are used as previously shown in 5.3.1.2.2.

Employee Name - Searches the "Employees" sheet and looks for the row that matches the Employee ID. It then brings in the particular employee's full name.

Employee Name	Hire Date	Incentives Earned YTD	Incentives Earned This Pay Period	Incentive Amount Earned This Pay Period	Current Pay Period Start
=INDEX({Employees | Employee Full Name}, MATCH([Employee ID]@row, {Employees | Employee ID}, 0))					

Hire Date - Searches the "Employees" sheet and looks for the row that matches the Employee ID. It then brings in the particular employee's hire date.

Hire Date	Incentives Earned YTD	Incentives Earned This Pay Period	Incentive Amount Earned This Pay Period	Current Pay Period Start	Cur Pay Enc
=INDEX({Employees | Hire Date}, MATCH([Employee ID]@row, {Employees | Employee ID}, 0))	1				

Incentives Earned YTD - Searches for rows in the "Incentives Earned" sheet that have a value in the "Employee ID" column matching the "Employee ID" column in this sheet as well as the year in the "Incentive Submitted Date" column matching the year calculated from the TODAY() function. Returns a sum from the "Amount" column in the "Incentives Earned" sheet for matching rows. This sum is the total amount of incentives the employee has earned year to date (YTD).

Incentives Earned YTD	Incentives Earned This Pay Period	Incentive Amount Earned This Pay Period	Current Pay Period Start	Current Pay Period End Date	Current Pay Period Pay Date	Today
=SUMIFS({Incentives Earned | Amount}, {Incentives Earned | Employee ID}, [Employee ID]@row, {Incentives Earned | Submitted Date}, YEAR(@cell) = YEAR(TODAY()))						

Incentives Earned This Pay Period - Searches the "Employees" sheet and looks for the row that matches the Employee ID. It then brings in the incentives earned by that particular employee.

Incentives Earned This Pay Period	Incentive Amount Earned This Pay Period	Current Pay Period Start	Current Pay Period End Date	Current Pay Period Pay Date	Today
=INDEX({Employees | Incentives}, MATCH([Employee ID]@row, {Employees | Employee ID}, 0))					

Incentive Amount Earned This Pay Period - Searches the "Employees" sheet and looks for the row that matches the Employee ID. It then brings in the dollar amount of the incentives earned by that particular employee.

Incentive Amount Earned This Pay Period	Current Pay Period Start	Current Pay Period End Date	Current Pay Period Pay Date	Today
=INDEX({Employees | Incentive Amount}, MATCH([Employee ID]@row, {Employees | Employee ID}, 0))				

5.3.2.2 Employee Dashboard

Finally, the individualized dashboard can be built. The data displayed on the dashboard will come from the "Employee File" sheet. Below is a sample of how the data can be presented on the dashboard.

🕐 **Employee Dashboard** ☆

Employee Details		Current Pay Period Important Dates	
Employee Name	Andrew Cencini	Current Pay Period Start	05/07/23
Employee ID	EID-0002	Current Pay Period End Date	05/20/23
Hire Date	06/13/22	Current Pay Period Pay Date	05/26/23

Incentives Earned	
Incentives Earned This Pay Period	Employee Referral
Incentive $ This Pay Period	$500.00
Incentive $ Earned YTD	$500.00

The purpose of this dashboard is to clearly display key data points about their employment in addition to pay period information and their individual incentives. All of the data is displayed using the dashboard widget type of "Metric Widget." This type of widget is great for displaying data that is not fit for displaying in a chart format.

5.3.2.3 Using the Template

How can the template for the employee dashboard be used in practice? The template folder is copied using the "Save as New" action. An easy way to access this action is to right click on the folder. A menu will be displayed and the "Save as New…" option can be chosen.

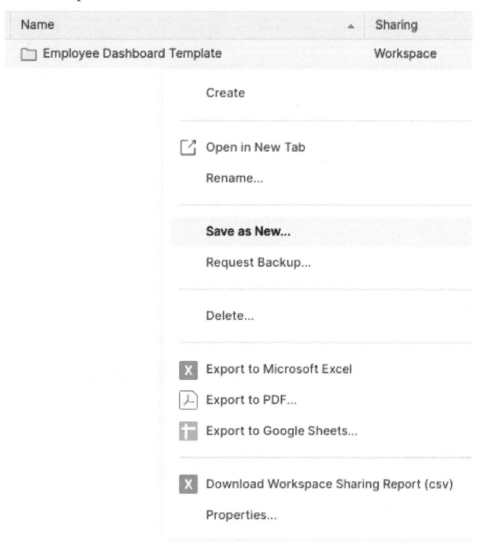

The new folder can then be named using the desired employee's name. For illustration purposes, we'll choose the employee Jan Kotas. Upon saving the template folder with her name, the sheet and dashboard can be renamed as well. Below is an example of what her folder will look like.

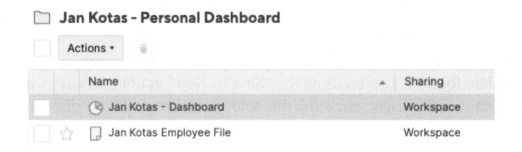

The sheet "Jan Kotas Employee File" is then updated with her Employee ID which is EID-0003. After updating the file with the corresponding Employee ID, all the rest of her information will be populated.

Employee ID	Employee Name	Hire Date	Incentiv... Earned YTD	Incentives Earned This Pay Period	Incentive Amount Earned This Pay Period	Current Pay Period Start	Current Pay Period End Date	Current Pay Period Pay Date	Today
EID-0003	Jan Kotas	12/05/22	$550.00	Project Completed Early	$50.00	05/07/23	05/20/23	05/20/23	05/06/23

And almost like magic, Jan's personalized dashboard will display all of the data from her employee file. In order for Jan to see her dashboard, she can be shared to the dashboard with viewer permissions.

🕐 **Jan Kotas - Dashboard** ☆

Employee Details		**Current Pay Period Important Dates**	
Employee Name	Jan Kotas	Current Pay Period Start	05/07/23
Employee ID	EID-0003	Current Pay Period End Date	05/20/23
Hire Date	12/05/22	Current Pay Period Pay Date	05/26/23

Incentives Earned	
Incentives Earned This Pay Period	Project Completed Early
Incentive $ This Pay Period	$50.00
Incentive $ Earned YTD	$550.00

5.3.3 Enhancing the *Gurus Unlimited* Solution

The example solution presented in this book works as is, but there are some areas where it can be enhanced. Here are a few examples of enhancements and how they could be implemented:

* ★ Additional reports and metrics

* ★ Automating the creation of the individualized employee dashboards

* ★ Preventing data entry errors

5.3.3.1 Additional Reports and Metrics

This solution as built provides opportunities for additional reports that would assist in the presentation of data and metrics. While no additional reports were identified during requirement gathering, a few examples of additional reports that would prove useful are:

* ★ A report showing active employees

* ★ A report showing active incentives

* ★ A report grouping incentives earned by employee

Not only would these reports provide an easy way to display a subset of the data, they could also be used to generate some easy metrics and answer questions such as:

* ★ How many employees are active?

* ★ How many incentives are available to be earned?

* ★ Which employees have earned the most incentives and how much?

The additional ways the data could be reported on and the metrics that could be generated are too numerous to attempt to list them all. However, these examples are very likely to add immediate value and answer some questions for key stakeholders in the *Gurus Unlimited* organization.

5.3.3.2 Automating Employee Dashboard Creation

The process for creating a new "Employee File" sheet and "Employee Dashboard" for each employee isn't too cumbersome, but it does take time. Moreover, when new employees are hired, there needs to be a process in place for someone to create the new Smartsheet items. What if there was a way that this could be automated when a new employee is added to the "Employees" sheet?

Smartsheet Control Center is an option to create the employee dashboards in an automated manner. Getting into too many specifics about Control Center is out of scope for this book, but it should be mentioned for completeness. Control Center has multiple options for creating Smartsheet items from a template, which is called a blueprint in Control Center. An example in the context of the Gurus Unlimited solution is that the "Employees" sheet can have a checkbox, that when checked, would trigger Control Center to create an "Employee File" and "Employee Dashboard" for a given employee.

5.3.3.3 Preventing Data Entry Errors

As built, the solution provides occasions where errors can be made in data entry. For example, when a manager is logging an incentive earned by an employee, they must enter the employee ID, but this is prone to errors if a character is forgotten or an extra character is added. It would be better if the manager could select the employee ID from a pre-populated dropdown list that is kept up to date with the active employees. While core Smartsheet does not have this functionality built in, there are several options. The same could be said for the "Incentive" column in the "Incentives Earned" sheet since the value entered here is taken from the "Employee Incentives List" sheet.

The list below is not exhaustive but includes some options for keeping the Employee ID in the "Incentives Earned" sheet in sync with the Employee ID's in the "Employees" sheet as well as the "Incentive" column in sync with the "Incentive ID" column in the "Employee Incentives List."

★ **Custom script to utilize Smartsheet's API:** This option can be time consuming and costly. If you have a team of developers or are proficient with a scripting language then you can tackle this yourself. The script will also need to be hosted on the web which can incur ongoing costs as well. The benefit of this approach is that you can tailor it to your exact needs.

★ **Smartsheet Data Shuttle:** Data Shuttle is a premium app offered by Smartsheet. It has many features, one being that you can update the options in a dropdown list from another data source, such as a Google Sheet or an attachment uploaded to a sheet in Smartsheet. If you already have access to this premium app, it may suit your needs. However, one limitation at this time is that it can't use a column in a sheet as the source for the dropdown list options.

★ **Smartsheet Bridge:** Smartsheet Bridge is an additional add-on service that can be used to integrate external systems with Smartsheet. Included in the feature set is the ability to update the options in a dropdown list from another sheet in Smartsheet. Your organization must have an Enterprise Smartsheet plan to use Smartsheet Bridge

★ **A dropdown list manager add-on:** Using an add-on such as the Dropdown List Manager offered by Smartsheet Guru avoids having to develop a solution to interact with Smartsheet's API and the solution can be set up quickly. Furthermore, it boasts the ability to not only use a sheet in Smartsheet as the source for the dropdown list options, but also a Smartsheet report!

 To learn more about the Dropdown List Manager, scan   the QR code or visit: smartsheetguru.com/dropdown

6

Documenting the Final Solution

Before building a solution you're going to collect requirements and map it out, right? What about after the solution is built? Should you have documentation of this as well? Of course! Unfortunately, creating good documentation of the solution that was developed is all too often an overlooked part of the architecture process. How common is it to not have good documentation? Very common. Usually, clients don't think about asking for this service. Furthermore, I've been hired to reverse engineer complex solutions that had no documentation. Usually, the situation is that a Smartsheet whiz will create a complex solution then leave a company without any of the solution being documented and no one else knows how it works.

At a minimum, document the workspaces, folders, the contents of each, and the automation workflows. Additionally, if you are using Smartsheet Control Center, Smartsheet premium apps, or integrating Smartsheet with third party applications then having an architecture document specific to each of those can be a good idea. To bring all of the pieces together, a high-level block diagram should be created to show how all the pieces interact at a high level and to show the flow of data between all of the elements. If you wish to provide an even greater level of detail, consider creating a how-to document explaining how to utilize the solution from start to finish.

6.1 Formatting the Documentation

What is the best format for the solution architecture documentation? A text-based document can be used to explain the workspaces and their structure. For automation workflows, a table works well for documenting the triggers and how they interact. Don't forget to create a visual diagram of the automation workflows as well as a diagram showing how data flows between all of the sheets, reports, dashboards, and outside elements.

6.2 *Gurus Unlimited* Solution Documentation

We will now create documentation for the *Gurus Unlimited* Smartsheet solution.

6.2.1 The Architecture Document

The architecture document will explain all of the Smartsheet items used to create the solution. It will explain each workspace, its organizational structure, and an explanation of each of the items. Let's create the content for the *Gurus Unlimited* architecture document.

A. **WORKSPACE**: Gurus Unlimited Administration - Contains the items that should be shared to solution administrators only.
   a. **FOLDER**: Employee Data
      i. **SHEET**: Employees - Contains the data on all employees.
   b. **FOLDER**: Incentives
      i. **SHEET**: Employee Incentives List - Contains the list of incentives and their status.
      ii. **SHEET**: Incentives Earned - Contains the list of incentives earned by each employee.
   c. **FOLDER**: Payroll
      i. **SHEET**: Biweekly Incentives Earned - Contains a historical record of the incentives earned each pay period.

     ii.   **SHEET**: Pay Period Metadata - Contains pay period data used in other sheets.

     iii.   **REPORT**: Payroll Report - Shows which incentives are due to be paid during the current pay period.

B. **WORKSPACE**: Gurus Unlimited Employee Dashboards - Contains the items needed for each unique employee dashboard.

    a. **FOLDER**: Employee Dashboard Template

     i.   **SHEET**: Employee File - Contains the data needed about an individual employee that will be displayed on their unique dashboard.

     ii.   **DASHBOARD**: Employee Dashboard - An individual employee's unique dashboard.

Since multiple items in this solution contain links to each other, let's show how each of the sheets, reports, and dashboards are related and how data flows between them. A visual diagram can be produced showing how data is linked between all of the items.

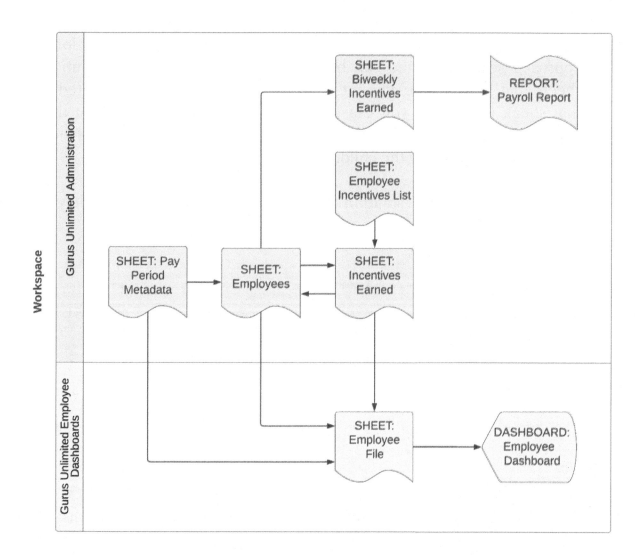

6.2.2 The Automation Workflow Documents

There are two parts to documenting the automation workflows in the solution.

* ★ Documenting each of the automations

* ★ Documenting the data flows for automations that support a process or
move data between sheets or external sources

6.2.2.1 Documenting the Automations

Documenting each of the automations can take different forms. Choose an
approach that makes sense for your use case and the complexity of the

solution. One approach I've used successfully is creating a table that lists the workflow by name along with its triggers, conditions, and actions. This approach scales well and can be used for simple to complex solutions. For sheets that have a large amount of workflows, a table can be created just for that sheet. Otherwise, you can use a single table and also include the sheet name on each row or use a hierarchical design with the sheet being the parent and the workflow being the children.

The *Gurus Unlimited* solution only has a few workflows, so they are all combined in one table.

Sheet Name	Workflow Name	Trigger	Conditions	Action
Employees	Copy Incentives Earned Biweekly	When the date in column 'Current Pay Period End' is reached at 10:00 PM	The value in the column 'Amount Incentives Earned Current Pay Period' is greater than 0	Copy rows to sheet "Biweekly Incentives Earned"
Pay Period Meta Data	Record Today's Date	Every day at 3:00 AM	N/A	Record a date in column 'Today'
Employee File	Record Today's Date	Every day at 3:00AM	N/A	Record a date in column 'Today'

Guru Move: Include a link along with the sheet name to easily navigate to the sheets that contain the workflows. (Not shown)

6.2.2.2 Documenting the Data Flows

Documenting the data flows resulting from automations is best documented using a flow diagram. Again, the exact format should make sense for your use case. The *Gurus Unlimited* solution only has one workflow that copies data between sheets. Here is an example of how the diagram could look.

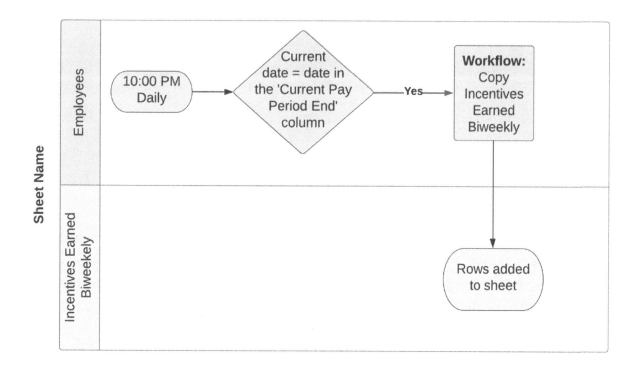

6.3 Storing the Documentation

Where to store the documentation depends on your organization's processes. If you have a dedicated document management system, then the documents can be stored there. Otherwise, consider storing the documentation right in Smartsheet! Take note of who should have access to the solution architecture documentation to help decide where to store it. For a single Smartsheet solution, adding the documentation to an administrative workspace or sheet can work well. However, if you have multiple solutions built out in your Smartsheet environment, consider creating a dedicated workspace for storing the documentation. Within this workspace, a sheet can reside that contains a row for each solution. Each row would then contain a description of the solution and all documentation would be attached to the row. A benefit of this approach is that the sheet or workspace can be shared with all users in the organization with view only permissions for easy access to the documentation, if that is desired.

Conclusion

Are you ready to take that ambitious idea you have to automate that outdated process? Great! You are well prepared to take on that project. The concepts you have acquired will allow you to create a roadmap to bring your Smartsheet project from idea to implementation!

If you haven't built out the example solution, I invite you to do that now to help solidify the concepts you have learned. Furthermore, please claim your bonus content if you have not done so already! Not only will you get the additional content to accompany this book, but we'll be able to connect through my Smartsheet-focused newsletter!

 To access your bonus content, scan the QR code or visit:

smartsheetguru.com/architecture-bonus

Thank You

Finally, thank you for reading this book. I'd really like to hear your feedback and I encourage you to send it to me at smartsheetguru.com/contact. If nothing else, please leave a review where you bought the book.

Additional Resources

Included in this section are additional resources as well as resources included through the book for your convenience.

Smartsheet Solution Architecture bonus content
smartsheetguru.com/architecture-bonus/

Smartsheet Guru's 7 Smartsheet Tips - A free guide of Smartsheet tips
smartsheetguru.com/tips

 Smartsheet Guru's debut eBook:
Smartsheet User Guide for Accelerated
Learning

smartsheetguru.com/userguide

 Process mapping and BPMN resources

smartsheetguru.com/process-mapping

 Smartsheet Guru's YouTube channel
providing tutorials and tips

smartsheetguru.com/youtube

 Learn more about Zoho Vault, for
storing account credentials

smartsheetguru.com/zohovault

Learn more about Lucidchart's process mapping features

smartsheetguru.com/lucidchart

Dropdown List Manager add-on

smartsheetguru.com/dropdown

List of approved domains for web content widgets

smartsheetguru.com/webwidgetshelp

About the Author

Darren Mullen grew up in New Orleans, Louisiana and moved to Tucson, Arizona after graduating from the University of New Orleans with a Bachelor of Science degree in Electrical Engineering. His Smartsheet journey began when he developed a solution in Smartsheet to manage parts obsolescence projects. This solution involved building a workflow tool in Smartsheet including developing scripts to utilize the Smartsheet API for custom use cases.

He then started his YouTube channel "Smartsheet Guru" and this helped him launch his own business, Smartsheet Guru, to provide Smartsheet and Appsheet consulting and coaching services. In December 2022, he published his first eBook, *Smartsheet User Guide for Accelerated Learning: Powerful Tips to Jump-Start Your Smartsheet Training*. In January 2023, he was named a Smartsheet Community Champion to recognize his contributions in the Smartsheet Community.

smartsheetguru.com

Made in the USA
Las Vegas, NV
18 October 2024

97057265R00044